This journal belongs to:

____

LUCKY SPROUT PRESS

THE TAROT CARD Journal

Table of Contents

Foreword

Within each of us, there lies a path that leads to a deep and powerful font of wisdom. No matter who you are, where you come from, or what you believe, you have the same access as everyone else to this vast knowledge. That's kind of wonderful, isn't it?

The tarot is just one of many tools that you can use to access this wisdom. The messages, images, and symbols prompted by these cards encourage us to draw out meaning from this internal reserve. The cards become so much more than a series of pretty images: they become a communication tool, encouraging dialogue between different sources.

Card reading can be a conversation between two people, or it can be a conversation between you and the spiritual world. It can also be a conversation between you and your inner self; the wise, trusting interior world that can sometimes be difficult to access in our busy, noisy world. There is nothing to fear when reading cards, tarot or otherwise; they only possess the power you give them. Everything originates from you.

Your ritual for reading cards can be completely custom for you. Take any advice on how you should work with your cards with a grain of salt. You can certainly take other people's practices as examples, but trust in your own intuition above all. If you need to set a perfect stage with candles, crystals, scents and sounds, go for it! But don't assume this is the only way to work with your cards and connect with your inner wisdom. A few deep breaths might be all the cleansing you need before starting to ask questions. Trust in yourself and in your intuition, and don't second guess when you feel urged to pick a certain card. There are no wrong choices!

The guiding principle behind so many spiritual practices - "do no harm" - is simple for a reason. As long as we act with the best of intentions and with kindness, we will see the same returned to us. Read your cards with an open mind and curiosity in your heart, and you will find the answers you seek.

I designed this journal to be a useful tool in anyone's tarot journey. Every card from the traditional tarot deck has its own two-page spread with room for your interpretations and notes. This will create a useful reference guide for you to consult as you pose questions to the cards. I believe it is very important that you build up your own definitions and meanings for each card, rather than solely relying on someone else's interpretations. These sorts of guides can be a great starting point, but you should listen to your own instincts about the meaning behind each image.

Each card's page has a space for notes on your feelings, keywords, and symbolism, as well as some blank space for extra notes. These are prompts to help you consider different ways of interpreting the image and message on each card. Start with your feelings when you look at one. Does it make you feel excited, worried, lonely, strong? Do you feel like it is a negative or positive card? Create your own rules for understanding each one.

Keywords could be any words that pop into your mind when you look at the art, the words, or the numbers on a card. This is helpful as a quick reference for later, especially if you're doing a reading for someone else. This is true for any symbolism that stands out to you, too. You can think about classic archetypes, myths or legends, or even pop culture references that remind you of a card. Whatever you associate with that image is completely valid and can help you to find answers.

If you're just getting started on your tarot reading journey, you might find it helpful to pick one card a day. Fill out its entry while studying it. This will allow you to really get to know your deck, and to appreciate the messages and wisdom that each card can draw from you.

The second half of this journal includes blank reading records. This is a space for you to keep track of the questions that you are asking, the cards you pull, and the way that you interpret these answers. You can keep track of all your readings, or just extra special ones - the choice is yours.

Intuitive card reading is a powerful tool to help you learn to see messages and intention everywhere. Though reading cards is a terrific solo activity, it's also a lot of fun to do with a community. Don't be afraid to seek out others who resonate with this practice. Whether you find kindred spirits where you live or online, seeing your intention to learn reflected in others is wonderfully affirming.

Have fun, do your best, and trust yourself!

Rebecca Wilson
Intuitive Reader and Author

The Fool
The Magician
The High Priestess
The Empress
The Emperor
The Hierophant
The Lovers
The Chariot
Strength
The Hermit
Wheel of Fortune
Justice
The Hanged Man
Death
Temperance
The Devil
The Tower
The Star
The Moon
The Sun
Judgement
The World

Major Arcana

Notes

The Fool

Feelings:

Keywords & Concepts:

Symbolism:

Notes

The Magician

Feelings:

Keywords & Concepts:

Symbolism:

Notes

The High Priestess

Feelings:

Keywords & Concepts:

Symbolism:

Notes

The Empress

Feelings:

Keywords & Concepts:

Symbolism:

Notes

The Emperor

Feelings:

Keywords & Concepts:

Symbolism:

Notes

The Hierophant

Feelings:

Keywords & Concepts:

Symbolism:

Notes

The Lovers

Feelings:

Keywords & Concepts:

Symbolism:

Notes

The Chariot

Feelings:

Keywords & Concepts:

Symbolism:

Notes

Strength

Feelings:

Keywords & Concepts:

Symbolism:

Notes

The Hermit

Feelings:

Keywords & Concepts:

Symbolism:

Notes

The Wheel of Fortune

Feelings:

Keywords & Concepts:

Symbolism:

Notes

Justice

Feelings:

Keywords & Concepts:

Symbolism:

Notes

The Hanged Man

Feelings:

Keywords & Concepts:

Symbolism:

Notes

Death

Feelings:

Keywords & Concepts:

Symbolism:

Notes

Temperance

Feelings:

Keywords & Concepts:

Symbolism:

Notes

The Devil

Feelings:

Keywords & Concepts:

Symbolism:

Notes

The Tower

Feelings:

Keywords & Concepts:

Symbolism:

Notes

The Star

Feelings:

Keywords & Concepts:

Symbolism:

Notes

The Moon

Feelings:

Keywords & Concepts:

Symbolism:

Notes

The Sun

Feelings:

Keywords & Concepts:

Symbolism:

Notes

Judgement

Feelings:

Keywords & Concepts:

Symbolism:

Notes

The World

Feelings:

Keywords & Concepts:

Symbolism:

Ace of Cups
2 of Cups
3 of Cups
4 of Cups
5 of Cups
6 of Cups
7 of Cups
8 of Cups
9 of Cups
10 of Cups
Page of Cups
Knight of Cups
Queen of Cups
King of Cups

Cups

Notes

Ace of Cups

Feelings:

Keywords & Concepts:

Symbolism:

Notes

2 of Cups

Feelings:

Keywords & Concepts:

Symbolism:

Notes

3 of Cups

Feelings:

Keywords & Concepts:

Symbolism:

Notes

4 of Cups

Feelings:

Keywords & Concepts:

Symbolism:

Notes

5 of Cups

Feelings:

Keywords & Concepts:

Symbolism:

Notes

6 of Cups

Feelings:

Keywords & Concepts:

Symbolism:

Notes

7 of Cups

Feelings:

Keywords & Concepts:

Symbolism:

Notes

8 of Cups

Feelings:

Keywords & Concepts:

Symbolism:

Notes

9 of Cups

Feelings:

Keywords & Concepts:

Symbolism:

Notes

10 of Cups

Feelings:

Keywords & Concepts:

Symbolism:

Notes

Page of Cups

Feelings:

Keywords & Concepts:

Symbolism:

Notes

Knight of Cups

Feelings:

Keywords & Concepts:

Symbolism:

Notes

Queen of Cups

Feelings:

Keywords & Concepts:

Symbolism:

Notes

King of Cups

Feelings:

Keywords & Concepts:

Symbolism:

Ace of Wands
2 of Wands
3 of Wands
4 of Wands
5 of Wands
6 of Wands
7 of Wands
8 of Wands
9 of Wands
10 of Wands
Page of Wands
Knight of Wands
Queen of Wands
King of Wands

Wands

Notes

Ace of Wands

Feelings:

Keywords & Concepts:

Symbolism:

Notes

2 of Wands

Feelings:

Keywords & Concepts:

Symbolism:

Notes

3 of Wands

Feelings:

Keywords & Concepts:

Symbolism:

Notes

4 of Wands

Feelings:

Keywords & Concepts:

Symbolism:

Notes

5 of Wands

Feelings:

Keywords & Concepts:

Symbolism:

Notes

6 of Wands

Feelings:

Keywords & Concepts:

Symbolism:

Notes

7 of Wands

Feelings:

Keywords & Concepts:

Symbolism:

Notes

8 of Wands

Feelings:

Keywords & Concepts:

Symbolism:

Notes

9 of Wands

Feelings:

Keywords & Concepts:

Symbolism:

Notes

10 of Wands

Feelings:

Keywords & Concepts:

Symbolism:

Notes

Page of Wands

Feelings:

Keywords & Concepts:

Symbolism:

Notes

Knight of Wands

Feelings:

Keywords & Concepts:

Symbolism:

Notes

Queen of Wands

Feelings:

Keywords & Concepts:

Symbolism:

Notes

King of Wands

Feelings:

Keywords & Concepts:

Symbolism:

Ace of Pentacles
2 of Pentacles
3 of Pentacles
4 of Pentacles
5 of Pentacles
6 of Pentacles
7 of Pentacles
8 of Pentacles
9 of Pentacles
10 of Pentacles
Page of Pentacles
Knight of Pentacles
Queen of Pentacles
King of Pentacles

Pentacles

Notes

Ace of Pentacles

Feelings:

Keywords & Concepts:

Symbolism:

Notes

2 of Pentacles

Feelings:

Keywords & Concepts:

Symbolism:

Notes

3 of Pentacles

Feelings:

Keywords & Concepts:

Symbolism:

Notes

4 of Pentacles

Feelings:

Keywords & Concepts:

Symbolism:

Notes

5 of Pentacles

Feelings:

Keywords & Concepts:

Symbolism:

Notes

6 of Pentacles

Feelings:

Keywords & Concepts:

Symbolism:

Notes

7 of Pentacles

Feelings:

Keywords & Concepts:

Symbolism:

Notes

8 of Pentacles

Feelings:

Keywords & Concepts:

Symbolism:

Notes

9 of Pentacles

Feelings:

Keywords & Concepts:

Symbolism:

Notes

10 of Pentacles

Feelings:

Keywords & Concepts:

Symbolism:

Notes

Page of Pentacles

Feelings:

Keywords & Concepts:

Symbolism:

Notes

Knight of Pentacles

Feelings:

Keywords & Concepts:

Symbolism:

Notes

Queen of Pentacles

Feelings:

Keywords & Concepts:

Symbolism:

Notes

King of Pentacles

Feelings:

Keywords & Concepts:

Symbolism:

Ace of Swords
2 of Swords
3 of Swords
4 of Swords
5 of Swords
6 of Swords
7 of Swords
8 of Swords
9 of Swords
10 of Swords
Page of Swords
Knight of Swords
Queen of Swords
King of Swords

Swords

Notes

Ace of Swords

Feelings:

Keywords & Concepts:

Symbolism:

Notes

2 of Swords

Feelings:

Keywords & Concepts:

Symbolism:

Notes

3 of Swords

Feelings:

Keywords & Concepts:

Symbolism:

Notes

Feelings:

Keywords & Concepts:

Symbolism:

Notes

Feelings:

Keywords & Concepts:

Symbolism:

Notes

6 of Swords

Feelings:

Keywords & Concepts:

Symbolism:

Notes

7 of Swords

Feelings:

Keywords & Concepts:

Symbolism:

Notes

8 of Swords

Feelings:

Keywords & Concepts:

Symbolism:

Notes

Feelings:

Keywords & Concepts:

Symbolism:

Notes

10 of Swords

Feelings:

Keywords & Concepts:

Symbolism:

Notes

Page of Swords

Feelings:

Keywords & Concepts:

Symbolism:

Notes

Knight of Swords

Feelings:

Keywords & Concepts:

Symbolism:

Notes

Queen of Swords

Feelings:

Keywords & Concepts:

Symbolism:

Notes

King of Swords

Feelings:

Keywords & Concepts:

Symbolism:

Use the following pages to
record your card readings
and keep track of any
important card pulls that
you may want to reference
later. There's no wrong
way to use it, so include as
much or as little detail as
you'd like.

Reading Records

<table>
<tr><td>Date:</td></tr>
</table>

<table>
<tr><td>Topic:</td></tr>
</table>

<table>
<tr><td>Questions:</td><td>Cards:</td></tr>
</table>

<table>
<tr><td>Interpretations:</td></tr>
</table>

<table>
<tr><td>Date:</td></tr>
<tr><td>Topic:</td></tr>
</table>

Questions:	Cards:

Interpretations:

<table>
<tr><td>Date:</td></tr>
</table>

<table>
<tr><td>Topic:</td></tr>
</table>

<table>
<tr><td>Questions:</td><td>Cards:</td></tr>
</table>

<table>
<tr><td>Interpretations:</td></tr>
</table>

<table>
<tr><td>Date:</td></tr>
<tr><td>Topic:</td></tr>
</table>

Questions:	Cards:

Interpretations:

Date:

Topic:

Questions:

Cards:

Interpretations:

Date:

Topic:

Questions:

Cards:

Interpretations:

Date:

Topic:

Questions:	Cards:

Interpretations:

Date:

Topic:

Questions:

Cards:

Interpretations:

<table>
<tr><td>Date:</td></tr>
</table>

<table>
<tr><td>Topic:</td></tr>
</table>

Questions:	Cards:

Interpretations:

Date:

Topic:

Questions:

Cards:

Interpretations:

Date:

Topic:

Questions:

Cards:

Interpretations:

Date:

Topic:

Questions:

Cards:

Interpretations:

Date:

Topic:

Questions:

Cards:

Interpretations:

Date:

Topic:

Questions:

Cards:

Interpretations:

<table>
<tr><td>Date:</td></tr>
<tr><td>Topic:</td></tr>
</table>

Questions:	Cards:

Interpretations:

<table>
<tr><td>Date:</td></tr>
</table>

<table>
<tr><td>Topic:</td></tr>
</table>

<table>
<tr><td>Questions:</td><td>Cards:</td></tr>
</table>

<table>
<tr><td>Interpretations:</td></tr>
</table>

<table>
<tr><td>Date:</td></tr>
<tr><td>Topic:</td></tr>
</table>

Questions:	Cards:

Interpretations:

<table>
<tr><td>Date:</td></tr>
</table>

<table>
<tr><td>Topic:</td></tr>
</table>

Questions:	Cards:

Interpretations:

Date:

Topic:

Questions:

Cards:

Interpretations:

| Date: |
| Topic: |

| Questions: | Cards: |

| Interpretations: |

Date:

Topic:

Questions:

Cards:

Interpretations: